ROCKFORD PUBLIC LIBRARY

3 1112 01776746 4

W9-BIA-774

J 796.75 HOL
Holter, James
Dirt bike racers

070110

WITHDRAWN

ROCKFORD PUBLIC LIBRARY

Rockford, Illinois

www.rockfordpubliclibrary.org

815-965-9511

DIRT-BIKE RACERS

James Holter

Enslow Publishers, Inc.
40 Industrial Road
Box 398
Berkeley Heights, NJ 07922
USA

http://www.enslow.com

ROCKFORD PUBLIC LIBRARY

Copyright © 2010 by Enslow Publishers, Inc.
All rights reserved.
No part of this book may be reproduced by any means without the written permission of the publisher.

Library of Congress Cataloging-in-Publication Data
Holter, James.
  Dirt bike racers / James Holter.
    p. cm. — (Kid racers)
  Includes bibliographical references and index.
  Summary: "High interest book for reluctant readers containing action packed photos and stories of the hottest dirt bikes and races for kids, discussing which motorcycles qualify, how they are built and raced, who the best drivers are, what to look for in a motorcycle, safety, good sportsmanship, and how racing activities can be a good part of family life"—Provided by publisher.
  ISBN 978-0-7660-3483-9
  1. Motorcycles, Racing—Juvenile literature. 2. Motorcycles—Juvenile literature. I. Title.
  GV1060.H65 2010
  796.7'5—dc22
                              2009020783

ISBN 978-0-7660-3752-6 (paperback)

Printed in the United States of America

102009 Lake Book Manufacturing, Inc., Melrose Park, IL

10 9 8 7 6 5 4 3 2 1

To Our Readers:
We have done our best to make sure all Internet addresses in this book were active and appropriate when we went to press. However, the author and the publisher have no control over and assume no liability for the material available on those Internet sites or on other Web sites they may link to. Any comments or suggestions can be sent by e-mail to comments@enslow.com or to the address on the back cover.

   Any stunts shown in this book have been performed by experienced riders and should not be attempted by beginners.

   ♻ Enslow Publishers, Inc., is committed to printing our books on recycled paper. The paper in every book contains 10% to 30% post-consumer waste (PCW). The cover board on the outside of each book contains 100% PCW. Our goal is to do our part to help young people and the environment too!

Adviser: *Mike Badalamenti, 25 years racing, Vet A/B (expert/intermediate)*

Cover Photo Credit: Digital Vision Ltd/SuperStock
Interior Photo Credits: Alamy/David Cattanach, p. 4; Alamy/Geoff Waugh, p. 18; Alamy/Anthony Arendt, p. 19; Alamy/Mario Moreno, p. 22; AP Photo/Jim Cole, p. 10; AP Photo/Jeff Roberson, p. 23; Corbis/Troy Wayrynen/NewSport, p. 7; Corbis/Ann Johansson, p. 11; Dreamstime.com/Lucian Coman, p. 16; Getty Images, p. 6; Getty Images/Wirelmage, pp. 14, 39; Marlene Hielema, p. 40; Courtesy of James Holter, pp. 1, 36; iStockphoto.com/Johann Sebastian Kopp, p. 5; iStockphoto.com/Greg McKay, p. 17; iStockphoto.com/W. R. Mayes, p. 31; iStockphoto.com/djjohn, p. 32; iStockphoto.com/Ivan Hafizov, pp. 42–43; Kardyphoto.Com/Jeff Kardas, pp. 25, 27, 35; ©2009 Kawasaki Motors Corp., U.S.A., p. 9, ©2007 Kawasaki Motors Corp., U.S.A., p. 12; Paul Martinez, p. 34; Photo Edit/Dennis MacDonald, p. 21; Photo Edit/Dennis MacDonald, p. 29; Photo Edit/Lon C. Diehl, pp. 30, 38; RoadAndDirt.Com/Gregg Brotman, pp. 24, 28, 37; Gary Semics MX School, www.gsmxs.com, p. 33; SuperStock/Corbis, p. 8; SuperStock/Creatas, p. 26; Matt Ware, p. 15; Courtesy of Yamaha Motor Corporation, U.S.A., p. 13.

Contents

1

Up to forty riders can start a motocross race at the same time. Ready . . . set . . . GO!

SPEED DEMONS ON DIRT

Forty racers are lined up side by side. They rev the engines on their dirt bikes. The riders lean over their handlebars and watch the metal starting gate. Their front wheels inch toward the gate with each blip of their throttles.

The gate drops! The racers fire off the line. Their front wheels lift off the ground as they battle for position down a long straightaway.

One rider enters the first turn ahead of the pack. His bike is sliding sideways, but he's in total control. As the leader completes the turn, he twists his throttle harder. He speeds over a large jump and leaps 30 feet down the track. The rest of the pack follows. Two, three, even four riders jump side by side. They all have the same goal: to win the motocross race.

Rough Riders

Motocross—also called MX—is a sport for racing off-road motorcycles. Riders complete several laps around a course of jumps, turns, hills, and bumps. The winner is the first to complete the assigned number of laps.

High-Jump Heroes

Gravity pulls you back to the ground when you jump into the air. Think how hard it would be to jump while holding a heavy dirt bike! To leap high, dirt bike racers have to go fast and ride over steep jumps.

Some professional dirt bike racers can jump 100 feet or more.

HISTORY: FROM DIRT BUMPS TO MONSTER JUMPS

Motocross racing started in England in the 1920s. Road motorcyclists wanted to see who could ride fastest on tough off-road terrain. On early motocross tracks, the only obstacles were bumps and hills like the ones in any farmer's field. These natural-terrain obstacles seem tame now. Back then they were intense!

Today, motocross tracks look very different. They still include natural-terrain obstacles, but they also have man-made jumps. Today's professional

A British army motocross rider gets a push during a race in 1939.

racers can fly 100 feet through the air off those jumps. Modern tracks also have whoop-de-dos, off-camber turns, and deep ruts.

In the summer, pros race in the American Motorcyclist Association (AMA) National Motocross Championship. In the winter, they ride in the AMA Supercross Championship. Motocross races happen outdoors. Supercross races are on man-made courses inside large stadiums. Supercross began in the 1970s. Since then, all the top riders have raced in both motocross and Supercross.

Dirt Bike Heroes

Famous dirt bike racers include Roger DeCoster from the 1960s, Bob Hannah from the 1970s, Rick Johnson and Jeff Ward from the 1980s, and Jeremy McGrath from the 1990s.

Today's Fastest Riders

Retired racer Ricky Carmichael (right) is considered the greatest motocross racer of all time. He has won the most national motocross championships in history. Today's top racers include James Stewart and Chad Reed. Stewart is the 2008 AMA Motocross and 2009 AMA Supercross champion. Reed is the 2008 AMA Supercross champion.

Kids as young as four—and adults of any age—can learn to ride motocross.

LEARNING TO RIDE

Learning to ride a motorcycle can be fun. The key is to have a good attitude. Don't ride too fast. Also, stay away from terrain that is too difficult for you or your motorcycle.

Before you can go fast or take big jumps, you need to learn the basics.

A motocross bike is powered by a gasoline engine. A twist throttle on the right handgrip controls the power of the engine. A clutch lever near the left handgrip controls how much of that power passes to the transmission. The front brake lever is near the right handgrip. The rear brake lever is near the right footpeg.

twist throttle

front brake lever

clutch lever

engine

rear brake lever

Be a Clutch Performer

One of the hardest controls to learn is the clutch. To practice, release the clutch slowly while turning the throttle slightly. When the motorcycle starts to edge forward, gently squeeze the clutch back in, close the throttle, and repeat.

Give Me a Brake!

A dirt bike in motion will tend to stay in motion. That's why the brakes are just as important as the throttle. Sometimes you will have to squeeze the brakes hard to slow down enough to turn at a corner.

SO YOU WANT TO BE A DIRT BIKE RACER?

After learning how to ride a dirt bike safely, many kids decide to race. Racing is fun and exciting. It tests your speed and skills against other riders. Motocross races are organized by adults. Races have rules to keep riders fair and safe.

You can be a dirt bike racer just about anywhere. These riders tackle a course at the Jolly Roger Moto-Sports Park in Lempster, New Hampshire.

When you race, your body and your motorcycle have to be prepared. Racing is tough—but with dedication, practice, and patience, anyone can become an MX racer.

Spotlight: Ashley Fiolek

One of today's best young dirt bike racers is eighteen-year-old Ashley Fiolek. Fiolek is a member of the American Honda Red Bull Racing factory team. She races in the Women's Motocross Association National Championship Series. At these events, she competes against the country's fastest female motocross racers.

How good is Fiolek? She is the 2008 WMA Motocross champion. She won the title in her first year as a pro!

Fiolek was successful as an amateur racer, too. Before she went pro, she won thirteen amateur national titles and more than a hundred races.

Here is another amazing fact about Fiolek: She is deaf. That doesn't slow her down, though! Fiolek overcomes her challenges by training hard and staying focused.

Ashley Fiolek is the first female athlete in history to join American Honda's Red Bull factory motocross race team.

Kawasaki makes dirt bikes for beginning riders. Their KLX models can grow with you as your skills improve.

BEGINNER BIKES

A beginner bike, or trail bike, is designed to be easy to ride. These motorcycles increase power more slowly than race bikes. Some beginner bikes have automatic clutches. They also have softer suspension. This means they travel more smoothly over small bumps.

Even the best riders learn to ride on beginner bikes. These bikes let new riders focus on learning the proper skills.

Beginner bikes are not built to handle big jumps, and they don't go as fast as race bikes. Do you want to go faster and jump farther? It's time to consider a race bike.

Noise Annoys!

Most beginner bikes are quiet. They come with exhausts that allow the bikes to be ridden on public trails.

Yamaha PW50

Find the Right Bike

There are many beginner bikes available today.

These bikes feature automatic clutches:
- Honda CRF50 and CRF70
- Yamaha PW50, TTR50, and TTR110
- Suzuki DR-Z70
- Kawasaki KLX110
- KTM 50 Mini Adventure

These bikes have manual clutches but are still easy to ride:
- Honda CRF80 and CRF100
- Yamaha TTR125
- Suzuki DR-Z125
- Kawasaki KLX140

RACE BIKES

Race bikes are designed for quick acceleration and high top speed.

Speed is the distance something travels in a set amount of time. Saying that a dirt bike goes "40 miles per hour" describes its speed. Acceleration is the rate of change of speed. For example, a dirt bike that accelerates fast builds speed quickly. For tracks with lots of corners and big jumps, fast acceleration is important. For flatter tracks with long, straight sections, high top speed is important.

The suspension on race bikes can handle large jumps. Race bikes are designed to be much lighter than beginner bikes.

Because they are built for high performance, race bikes cost more money than beginner bikes. They also need more maintenance.

At professional MX events, riders use top race bikes.

Race Bikes Allowed

Race bikes are designed for closed-course tracks, like Loretta Lynn's track above. They are not allowed on trails. They are too loud, and small sparks from their exhausts could start a fire.

Too Much Bike?

Some smaller race bikes have automatic clutches. They should not be mistaken for beginner bikes, though. These race bikes are still very fast and unsafe for beginners.

These race bikes have automatic clutches:
- KTM 50SX
- Cobra CX50
- Polini X1R and X3R

These race bikes have manual clutches:
- Kawasaki KX65 and KX85
- KTM 65SX, 85SX, and 105SX
- Suzuki RM85
- Yamaha YZ85
- Honda CR85 and CRF150R

Safety is the word no matter where you ride your bike. This racer is all geared up for the Kalahari Desert Race in Botswana, Africa.

GEAR UP FOR SAFETY

Without safety gear, you are more likely to get seriously hurt in a motocross race. Almost all track owners require safety equipment. Even if you only ride in your own backyard, you should always protect yourself.

The most important piece of safety gear is a helmet. You'll need protective eye goggles, boots, kneepads, and gloves. Most riders also wear elbow pads, riding pants, a riding jersey, a chest protector, and a neck brace.

Dirt bike riders never intend to crash, but they all take a spill or two. Safety gear protects you when you crash. Even slow crashes hurt!

Tight Is Right

A helmet must fit snugly on your head. A loose helmet will slide around as you ride. It won't protect your head if you crash.

Absorbing the Blow

A chest protector provides extra padding around your chest and back. Some chest protectors are

A snug helmet keeps you safe, and goggles keep mud out of your eyes.

large plastic guards that fit over your jersey. Others are small, light foam pads that you wear next to your skin.

Test Your Gear

Buy your first set of safety gear from a local motorcycle dealer, rather than ordering it online or by mail. That way, you can try the gear on to make sure it fits comfortably. The dealer also can answer questions about different brands and types of gear.

17

CAUTION ON THE COURSE

Athletes can get hurt playing any sport. Motocross is no different. Riding a motorcycle fast over jumps, hills, and bumps is fun. It also can be dangerous if you aren't careful.

The rider is most responsible for his or her own safety. It is important to know how fast you can ride safely and to ride within those limits. If you ride within your limits, chances are you will not crash.

A motocross rider gets covered in sand when he wipes out at a race in Somerset, England.

Don't Push It!

Know the limits of your motorcycle. Do not ride in places where it cannot go. Do not ride it faster than it should go.

Not all terrain is safe for riding. Be very careful in areas with cliffs, rocks, loose riding surfaces such as gravel, and steep hillsides.

Passing the Hard Way

Some of the worst crashes happen when MX riders collide. You should always keep a safe distance from other riders. When you are racing, be careful as you pass other riders. If you are being passed, do not make any sudden moves that might cause a crash.

Loose, uneven terrain pushes your riding skills to the limit. Here, a racer splashes through mud at the Lake Elsinore Grand Prix in California.

CRASH TALES

Everybody crashes sooner or later. Just follow these two tips, and you'll be fine. First, prepare for the worst by using safety gear. Second, when a crash does happen, learn from it.

Noah and the Jump

Noah, a kid racer from Ohio, had been riding and racing for many years. He and his dad went to a practice day at a new track. His first time around the track, Noah crashed on a jump. He was going too fast when he hit it.

"I did not learn the new track before I tried to go fast," Noah said. "I should have ridden the track slowly first so I would know what to expect when I hit the jump going fast."

All motocross tracks are different. It is very important to ride them slowly. Then you will know how they are laid out before you speed up.

Elliot and the Whoop-de-dos

Elliot, also from Ohio, was new to dirt bike racing. He went to a race with his brother and dad. In his second race of the day, Elliot crashed in the whoop-de-dos. He wasn't hurt, but he broke the brake lever on his XR70.

"I was not going straight when I hit the whoop-de-dos," Elliot said. "I was riding at an angle when I hit the first bump, and I lost control of my motorcycle."

To stay safe on the track, riders need to look ahead. You can't prepare for an obstacle if you don't know it's coming.

As these racers ride over whoop-de-dos, they try to keep their bikes as straight as possible.

Sand is a common surface for motocross tracks. It can make quite a spray, especially if it's dry!

TIME TO RIDE

Motocross tracks are not as common as baseball fields or basketball courts. Luckily, it can be easy to find a place to ride if you know where to look. Start by talking to people who work at a motorcycle dealership near your home. They can tell you about local tracks.

You also can find tracks by searching online. Ask your parents to help you look up local tracks and riding areas. Then give the tracks a call. Find out when they are open and how much they charge to ride.

All Tracks Are Different

Some tracks are sandy, while others have hard-packed dirt. Some tracks have big hills. Some are built in flat fields.

Ride with the Right Crowd

Some tracks have special times for smaller motorcycles and young riders to be on the track. If you ride a smaller dirt bike, it's dangerous to share the track with full-size motorcycles.

Conditions Matter

Some track owners take time to prepare their tracks during the day. They water the track to keep down the dust. Then the staff uses heavy machinery to smooth out the track's surface.

The 2008 AMA Supercross Series was held at this carefully built track at the Edward Jones Dome in St. Louis, Missouri.

TIME TO RACE!

The race day scene at a motocross track is fast paced and exciting. The pits are packed with riders on all sizes of bikes. They are hustling to get to the starting line or coming off the track, exhausted from their last race.

A lot happens on race days. All the events are well organized. For example, you are only allowed on the track at certain times. The track

This scene shows a well-organized race day. Racers must drive slowly in the parking area. In the background, a family is camping in their RV.

24

is well prepared. The dirt is watered to keep dust down, and the track crew smoothes out ruts between races.

There are often additional safety rules on race day. For example, signs tell you where and when you're allowed to ride your dirt bike. Make sure you follow these rules, or you might be asked to leave the track.

Home Court Advantage

It is a good idea to race at tracks where you have practiced. Then you will be familiar with the track.

Your Ad Here

You will notice a lot of new signs on race day. Companies pay the track owner to put up their signs. This advertises their services and products to the racers and fans.

Sponsors pay big money to place their signs at the AMA Amateur Motocross Nationals at Loretta Lynn's. This is one of the most respected amateur motocross events in the world.

12

A young racer sprays the chain of his dirt bike so its parts will work well.

A FINE-TUNED BIKE

If you don't keep your motorcycle in good shape, it will not perform at the top of its game. You have to learn how to maintain your dirt bike.

The most important tool for taking care of your bike is the manufacturer's service manual.

The service manual tells you how to keep your machine running strong.

Some maintenance jobs require special tools and knowledge. For these jobs, take your motorcycle to your local dealership.

One Size Fits All?

Modern motorcycles have different suspension, engine, and control settings. This means you can set up your bike just the way you like it without spending more money. Make sure you ask an adult for help whenever you work on your motorcycle.

Jazz It Up!

Working on your motorcycle isn't just about maintenance. There are many products that you can add to your dirt bike to make it cooler. Most dirt bike racers buy special sticker kits for their bikes. Some buy brightly colored plastic fenders.

This racer has put together an entire MX style, with decals, a matching outfit, and colorful gloves and helmet.

THE FIRST STEPS TO SPEED

Riding a motorcycle quickly and safely takes practice. Let's start with the basics.

The most important riding skill is cornering. When you corner, you must be smooth with your throttle. If you turn your throttle too quickly, your rear tire will spin. As you go through the corner, lean your motorcycle in the direction you are turning.

MX racers must be careful to judge the terrain as they corner, or take turns. They stick out their feet to keep their balance.

Hills are a common MX obstacle. Traction is different when you are going uphill. You need to lean forward to keep from flipping over backward. If you lean forward too far, your rear wheel can spin.

Motocross tracks develop a lot of ruts. Most ruts form in the corners. When you ride through a rut, stay smooth

Hills are a challenge for any MX racer.

and steady. If you make any sudden shifts in direction, you can fall over.

Be a Corner Master

Dirt bike riders often stick out their inside legs when they go around a corner. This riding position actually helps with balance as they lean the bike over. Another trick is to press down on the outside footpeg. This gives you better traction.

Start Me Up!

To get a good start, watch the starting gate closely. Gently let out your clutch until your motorcycle barely nudges forward as you turn the throttle. When the gate drops, turn the throttle quickly—but not so fast that your front wheel lifts too high off the ground.

14

TAKING IT TO THE NEXT LEVEL

Today's motocross tracks are filled with tough obstacles. If you want to win the race, you have to ride over these obstacles safely and quickly.

The fastest way over an obstacle is not always the safest. However, the safest way is not always the fastest! The best riders find a balance between safety and speed. This helps them get ahead of the pack and stay there.

Finding that balance takes a lot of practice. That's why you should always start slowly and then build up to trying

What's the most advanced obstacle? How about a jump over a track filled with other riders?

difficult terrain. Practice each type of obstacle many times before you move on to the next one. This is a good way to gain confidence.

All Whooped Up

Some whoop-de-dos are small. Other whoop-de-dos are as large as small jumps. The most important thing is to hit them straight. If you hit them at an angle, it will be hard to keep a steady speed.

Air Time

When you hit a jump, stand up and lean forward slightly. Be steady with the throttle. If you turn your throttle too hard, you can flip over backward. If you cut your throttle before you jump off the top, you can flip forward.

Freestyle riders are known for their high-flying stunts.

Jump Types

There are different types of jumps. On a single jump, you land on flat ground. On a double jump, you land on the backside of a second jump. A tabletop is like a double jump, but the space between the two jumps is filled in with dirt.

15

It's never too early to start MX school.
This student is just six years old.

GET SCHOOLED

Do you want to go faster on your dirt bike? Don't spend a lot of money to make your motorcycle faster. Instead, go to a riding school to make *yourself* go faster. Expert racers will teach you how to corner and jump the proper way. They will talk about the right attitude and training habits for racing.

Most riding schools are well organized. The trainers have been riding for many years, and they know the best ways to go fast on a motocross track. You can learn a lot from videos and books, but the best advice comes from one-on-one instruction.

Training for All Levels

There are riding schools for all experience levels. Beginner schools teach you the basics. Advanced schools cover more difficult techniques.

The Next Best Thing to Being There

Professional trainers sell books and videos that demonstrate the best riding methods. Gary Semics has been training both new and experienced riders since 1985. He has produced many books and videos on his techniques.

Students at the Gary Semics MX School can take individual or group lessons.

Racer Turned Teacher

Rick Johnson was one of the fastest motocross racers ever. He now helps run Rick Johnson's MX School of Champions. At the school, he teaches the skills that helped him win seven AMA National Motocross Championships.

RACING BY THE RULES

Most American racetracks use rules that are written by the AMA. This is helpful when you travel to different tracks. Wherever you race, you will follow the same rules.

The rules of dirt bike racing cover these areas:

- the sizes of bikes that are allowed to race each other
- the ages of riders who are allowed to race each other
- the skill level of riders who are allowed to race each other
- how riders are allowed to modify their bikes to make them faster
- how riders advance to higher skill levels
- safety guidelines for track owners

An AMA official holds up a sign during a pro race. Founded in 1924, the AMA is headquartered in Pickerington, Ohio.

Bending the Rules

"Outlaw" races are races that are not run using AMA rules. These races are not really illegal. The term dates back to before the AMA started organizing races. At that time, many races were held on public streets. Those races really were against the law.

Find a Race

AMA motocross races are listed on the AMA Web site. They are also published in the AMA magazine, which is mailed to members every month.

Future Champions

The top kid racers in the country face off every summer at the AMA Amateur Motocross Nationals in Hurricane Mills, Tennessee. Riders have to qualify to go to this race.

Amateur racers take their first turn at the AMA Nationals in Tennessee.

If you get nervous on race day, remember that dirt bike riding is about having fun.

RACE DAY RUNDOWN

On race day, you will be eager to get right on the track. You'll have to take a few first steps before you're set to ride.

As soon as you get to the track, you will go to the sign-up booth. Here you will choose your classes and pay your entry fee. There is usually a long line, so try to arrive early. You might even be able to sign up online before race day.

Shortly after sign-up closes, there will be a riders' meeting. Race officials will give you your practice group and race order. Then it will be time to hit the track for practice. Pay close attention to how the track has changed since you last rode there. Also, try taking the obstacles in different ways to find the fastest line.

Two Races, One Score

The most common structure for a motocross race is a two-moto format. In a two-moto format, each class has two races. Each rider's combined score from the two motos determines his or her overall score. After all classes have raced both motos, trophies are awarded.

Action Packed

Race days are packed with tons of action off the track. Vendors sell everything from T-shirts to dirt bike parts. Fans line the fences to cheer on their friends and favorite riders.

When you're done racing, how about a little shopping?

PIRELLI
competizioni

POWER IS NOTHING WITHOUT CONTROL

FAMILY TIME

Lots of kids go to dirt bike races, even if they don't race. They might be the brothers and sisters of the kids who do race. They come to watch, to hang out, and to cheer on their friends and family members.

Racing is a team effort. It's hard for a racer to win without strong support. Parents and siblings work on the bike, keep the gears and parts organized, and cheer loudly from the stands.

In some families, though, everyone races. A brother and sister might compete against each other on the track. Then they run back to the sidelines to cheer on Mom or Dad.

A father and his son pose with their motorcycles.

They Have Your Back

There will be times when the challenges of racing catch up to you. There will be broken parts on your motorcycle, banged-up parts on your body, and disappointing losses. It is much easier to overcome all of these challenges with the help and support of your family and friends.

Off the Track

Most families that race also go on trail rides. This is a great way for family members of all ages and skill levels to spend time together. Watching each other race is great, but riding together can be even better.

Strong Bonds

Some families stick together even after riders advance to the professional ranks. Mike and Jeff Alessi are brothers. They grew up riding as a team. Now they compete against each other as pro motocrossers.

Mike Alessi celebrates a win at the 2005 AMA Motocross Championship in Mt. Morris, Pennsylvania.

39

The beginning of a hare scrambles race looks exactly like its name: a scramble!

OTHER TYPES OF DIRT BIKE RACING

Motocross is not the only type of dirt bike racing. Other races are held in the woods or on flat, oval tracks.

All types of dirt bike racing have a few things in common, though. First, the races happen on the dirt. Second, racers almost always ride on motocross bikes that they have changed to fit their type of racing. Third, the races are all great fun!

Dirt Bikes Go Cross-Country

Hare Scrambles

A hare scrambles is a race of several laps around a marked trail in the woods. Hare scrambles bikes often have hand guards, soft suspension, and bash plates. These plates protect the bottom of the engine from rocks.

Dirt Track

Dirt track is a race around an oval-shaped course. Racers go counterclockwise, so they make only left turns. Dirt track bikes have smoother tires and are often lowered to better handle high speeds on long straightaways.

TT Racing

TT racing is like dirt track. However, the course has at least one right turn and one jump.

Hillclimb

In hillclimb, riders see who can make it up a hill the fastest. If no one makes it to the top, the racer who gets the farthest wins. Hillclimb bikes often have longer swingarms, which are parts that support the rear wheel.

THE ENVIRONMENT MATTERS

Dirt bike tracks and trails are almost always outside. Most of them are built in the country or in the woods. If you ride your dirt bike responsibly, you will not harm nature. If you are irresponsible, however, you can damage the planet.

Responsible riding protects the future of dirt bike racing. If riders damage the environment, they might not be allowed to use public land. Even private tracks might be closed down.

DO NOT use your dirt bike in these irresponsible ways:

- riding off the proper track or trail
- riding on trails without a spark arrestor
- riding a loud racing bike anywhere but on a closed-course track
- making ruts with your bike by spinning the rear tire on purpose

This dirt bike rider is being friendly to the environment. He is riding in a wide-open space on a dirt trail. This lowers his impact on land and wildlife.

Few sports give kids as much freedom and control as dirt bike riding. And racing is as extreme and exciting as a sport can get. The choices you make as a dirt bike rider can play a big role in protecting the future of the sport.

Protecting Your Right to Ride

Several organizations encourage responsible dirt bike riding. These include the American Motorcyclist Association, the Blue Ribbon Coalition, the National Off-Highway Vehicle Conservation Council, and Americans for Responsible Recreational Access.

GLOSSARY

acceleration—The rate at which an object's speed increases.

American Motorcyclist Association (AMA)—An organization that oversees street and off-road motorcycling and protects the rights of motorcyclists. It also makes rules for most amateur motorcycle racing in the United States. The AMA has about 300,000 members.

bash plates—Thick metal plates that protect a motorcycle engine from rocks.

closed-course tracks—Tracks that are restricted to a specified area, usually away from woods and neighborhoods.

clutch—A part that controls how much energy from the engine passes to the transmission. When the clutch is fully engaged, all the engine's energy passes to the transmission. When the clutch is disengaged, no energy passes to the transmission. When the clutch is partially engaged, only some of the engine's energy passes to the transmission.

cornering—Riding a dirt bike around a turn on a racetrack.

exhausts—Pipes that carry fumes from a motorcycle's engine into the air.

natural-terrain obstacles—Obstacles that result from natural changes in the earth, such as hills, drop-offs, and dips.

neck brace—A device that fits between a helmet and a person's shoulders. It keeps your neck from bending too far in any direction if you crash.

off-camber turns—Turns where the ground slopes in the opposite direction of the turn. For example, in a left-hand turn, the ground would slope toward the right.

pits—Areas around a racetrack where riders park and wait for a race to start.

race classes—Groups of racers organized by age, experience, and/or motorcycle size. Each class is scored separately.

ruts—Ditches created in the dirt by dirt bike tires.

spark arrestor—A part of a motorcycle's exhaust that prevents sparks from coming out.

straightaway—A section of a track that doesn't have any turns.

suspension—The parts of a dirt bike that soak up bumps and landings from big jumps.

swingarms—Straight pieces of steel or aluminum that connect the rear wheel to the rest of a motorcycle.

throttles—Devices that control the speed of a motorcycle.

traction—The ability to grip a surface.

transmission—The gears inside a motorcycle that determine how much of the engine's energy it takes to turn the rear wheel. You shift through the gears using a small lever by your left foot. In lower gears, the motorcycle accelerates quickly but has a low top speed. In higher gears, the motorcycle accelerates slowly but has a high top speed. The rider shifts gears to maintain the best acceleration and speed for the terrain.

whoop-de-dos—Series of bumps on a motocross track.

FURTHER READING

Books

Amick, Bill. *Motocross America.* St. Paul, Minn.: Motorbooks, 2005.

Armentrout, David, and Patricia Armentrout. *Dirt Bikes.* Vero Beach, Fla.: Rourke Pub., 2006.

David, Jack. *Dirt Bikes.* Minneapolis, Minn.: Bellwether, 2008.

Gorr, Eric. *Mini Motocross and Pit Bike Performance Handbook.* St. Paul, Minn.: Motorbooks, 2008.

Johnson, Ben. *Motocross.* New York: Crabtree Pub. Co., 2008.

Kalman, Bobbie, and John Crossingham. *Extreme Motocross.* New York: Crabtree Pub. Co., 2004.

Woods, Bob. *Motocross History from Local Scrambling to World Championship MX to Freestyle.* New York: Crabtree Pub. Co., 2008.

Web Sites

American Motorcyclist—*The official Web site of the American Motorcyclist Association*
<www.americanmotorcyclist.com>

MX Sports—*News about the qualifiers and championship races for the AMA Amateur Motocross Nationals*
<www.mxsports.com>

Off-road.com—*Bike reviews and tips for racing your dirt bike*
<www.off-road.com>

Women's Motocross Association (WMA)—*Read about ladies-only events, stars, and race results*
<www.womensmotocrossassociation.com>

INDEX